BILL GATES

BILL GATES

Software King
by John Wukovits

A Book Report Biography
FRANKLIN WATTS
A Division of Grolier Publishing
New York / London / Hong Kong / Sydney
Danbury, Connecticut

Cover illustration by Dave Kaboe, interpreted from a photograph by ©
Corbis Sygma/Rystedt

Photographs ©: AP/Wide World Photos: 67 (Sal Veder); Archive Photos:
72, 114 (Jeff Christensen/Reuters), 82 (Victor Malafronte), 23 (Jeff
Vinick/Reuters); Corbis Sygma: 88 (Darryl Heikes), 12 (Bill Chan), 108
(P. Durand), 84 (Grant Haller/Seattle Post Intelligencer), cover (Rystedt);
Corbis-Bettmann: 33; George White: 86; Globe Photos: 90 (Walter Weiss-
man); Liaison Agency, Inc.: 98 (Evan Agostini), 94 (Jeff Christensen), 111
(Scott Eklund), 75, 76 (Dirck Halstead), 70 (Kashi), 47 Olivier Laude), 101
(Brad Markel), 43 (Microsoft), 21 (A. Summa); Microsoft Archives: 2, 10,
36, 40, 50, 59, 63, 65; Seattle Post-Intelligencer: 52.

Visit Franklin Watts on the Internet at:
http://publishing.grolier.com

Library of Congress Cataloging-in-Publication Data

Wukovits, John.
Bill Gates : software king / by John Wukovits
    p.   cm.—(Book report biographies)
Includes bibliographical references and index.
ISBN 0-531-11669-7 (lib. bdg.) 0-531-16491-8 (pbk.)
1. Gates, Bill, 1955– 2. Microsoft Corporation—History. 3. Businessmen—
United States—Biography. 4. Computer software industry—United
States—History. I. Title. II. Book report biography.

HD9696.63.U62 G378 2000
338.7'610053'092—dc21
[B]   99-059372

CONTENTS

BILL GATES

CHAPTER ONE

THE START OF MICROSOFT

Paul Allen stared in astonishment at the January 1975 issue of *Popular Electronics* magazine. The headline proclaimed a new product called the Altair 8800, which the magazine described as the "World's First Minicomputer Kit to Rival Commercial Models." The accompanying article opened with the prediction that "the era of the computer in every home—a favorite topic among science fiction writers—has arrived!"

Allen quickly read through the article, which explained that a company called Micro Instrumentation and Telemetry Systems (MITS) in Albuquerque, New Mexico, had developed the first computer for the home market—the Altair 8800. Previously, only high-priced computers designed for businesses had been available, but now MITS's founder, Ed Roberts, appeared to have

The Altair 8800

created a machine that families and individuals could afford.

Computer devotees and electronics buffs embraced the Altair 8800, even though it contained significant flaws. For $400 the customer received a kit which, after laborious assembly, produced a computer with blinking lights, but without the capacity to perform any function. Since the operating system—the series of commands that coordinates a computer's components—used up the machine's entire amount of memory, the Altair 8800 could do nothing but sit on a desk and look impressive. It was as if a car had been developed, shiny engine and all, but with no driver to guide it up and down roads. In spite of this drawback, however, the computer found a ready market.

Allen stood at the newsstand in Harvard Square and showed the article to his friend and fellow computer enthusiast, Bill Gates. Like Allen, Gates immediately recognized that the Altair 8800 was only the first step, that soon someone would discover a way to make the home computer useful to consumers. Gates concluded that the Altair 8800 required a system of commands telling it what to do—a driver, in other words. The first person to develop such software would have a huge advantage over competitors, because home computers would then have a practical use.

Gates wanted to be that first person, but the problem demanded full-time effort. He would have to drop out of college to do it and he was only in his sophomore year at Harvard University. Doubts flooded his mind. Would his parents object? If he left Harvard, would he ever return? What if he tried to develop software but failed? On the other hand, should he hesitate now, his chance might disappear forever. As Paul Allen

*Melinda and Bill Gates and Paul Allen at a
recent basketball game*

reminded him, "If we don't do this, somebody else
is going to."

Gates needed little prodding. As *Biography
Today* reported, Gates explained, "We realized
that the [computer] revolution might happen
without us. After we saw that article, there was
no question of where our life would focus."

GATES DESIGNS BASIC

Gates and Allen bluffed their way through the
next stage. Though they had not put one

moment's labor into the project, they wrote a letter to Ed Roberts stating that they had devised a simple computer programming language called BASIC—Beginners' All-purpose Symbolic Instruction Code—that would enable the Altair 8800 to perform computations and do word processing. Later in Gates's career this tactic of announcing the existence of a product before its creation would be labeled "vaporware," but the strategy worked on Roberts.

Roberts recognized that if BASIC worked, the demand for his product would soar, so he telephoned the number printed on the stationery letterhead. The phone number happened to be that of Paul Gilbert, a friend who had worked with Gates on another project. When Paul's mother answered the phone and claimed that she knew nothing about the matter, Roberts almost let the idea drop.

However, Gates and Allen called Roberts back. After a brief discussion with him, the pair agreed to have their program ready for testing in about one month. Paul Allen recalls that when they hung up the phone, Gates glanced at him and said, "God, we gotta get going on this!"

The next month flew by as the two young men tried to create a computer programming language from scratch. Since they did not own an Altair 8800 and could hardly ask Roberts for one after they had already claimed to have created a language that worked for the machine—Allen hurriedly wrote a program which enabled Harvard's huge computer to imitate the Altair. As Gates later said to *People* magazine, "We just had this book that described the machine. If we had read the book wrong, or the book was wrong, we were hosed."

For the next five weeks Gates and Allen worked around the clock in Gates's dormitory room and in Harvard's computer lab to revise BASIC. Often, Gates fell asleep at the computer, awoke and resumed his work without even leaving the building. As he wrote in his 1995 book, *The Road Ahead*, "Sometimes I rock back and forth or pace when I'm thinking, because it helps me to focus on a single idea and exclude distractions. I did a lot of rocking and pacing . . . the winter of 1975. Paul and I didn't sleep much and lost track of night and day. When I did fall asleep, it was often at my desk or on the floor. Some days I didn't eat or see anyone. But after five weeks, our BASIC was written—and the world's first microcomputer software company was born."

"It was the coolest program I ever wrote."

Gates, who said, "It was the coolest program I ever wrote," had created the world's first language to command a personal computer (PC). All they had to do now was take it to Albuquerque and hope the program worked on the real Altair 8800.

TRIAL RUN ON THE ALTAIR 8800

Since Paul Allen looked older than the youthful-appearing Gates, he went to New Mexico to meet Ed Roberts. Even aboard the aircraft Allen added final touches to the program, and when the plane landed in Albuquerque he was still wondering whether their creation would work.

Both Roberts and Allen received a shock when they first met. Allen assumed MITS was a huge corporate entity with impressive home offices, but Roberts drove up in a dirty, dented pickup truck. The "home offices" proved to be little more than a small rented room in a strip mall.

Roberts felt just as uneasy. He expected Allen to be much older. His fears did not lessen when Allen said that he did not have enough money to pay for the hotel room that Roberts reserved. The head of MITS paid for the room, but it was hardly a promising beginning.

The next morning, Allen loaded his program into Roberts's Altair 8800 and anxiously waited for the computer to issue a response. For fifteen nerve-wracking minutes Allen and Roberts stared at the teletypewriter before a reply emerged: "Memory size?" Paul entered the amount of memory needed to complete the operation, then typed in the command, "PRINT 2 + 2."

He knew their futures rested upon the next few moments. If the computer responded successfully, he and Gates would have their first customer and their computer software company would be launched. Should it fail, he would return to Harvard with nothing to show but five wasted weeks of effort. Their dreams could dissipate in a few disastrous seconds.

In what seemed ages, the Altair 8800 accepted the command, then finally printed the correct answer, "4." A delighted Roberts said that he was prepared to strike a deal with his younger associates. Allen knew he and Gates would accept Roberts's proposal, but before agreeing to anything, Allen returned to Harvard to share the news with Gates.

GATES AND ALLEN FORM MICROSOFT

Back at Harvard, Allen and Bill Gates celebrated with ice cream and sodas and began planning their future. Fortunately, Gates foresaw that as the computer industry expanded, each computer maker would require its own version of BASIC to work with its PC. So when they closed their deal with Ed Roberts, Gates and Allen retained the rights to sell BASIC to any other company they chose.

Eventually, this could mean a huge roster of clients as well as fabulous profits. To realize this, however, Gates could not juggle the demands of both Harvard and a full-time business. By the spring of 1975, Paul Allen had already left his programming job with Honeywell, and Gates decided he would have to place his college career on hold.

At first, his parents were not happy with his decision. In the hope of keeping her son in school, Mary Gates set up a luncheon date with a family friend who had done well in industry. But the move backfired. The friend, a self-made millionaire who also had dropped out of college, listened avidly as Bill Gates described his plans and why he believed that software was the wave of the future. Instead of convincing Gates to remain in school, the family friend advised him to charge ahead with his dreams.

When his parents saw that nothing would deter their son, they gave him their full blessings. Gates left Harvard in June 1975 after his sophomore year, and later described the incident in his book, *The Road Ahead*. "They saw how much I wanted to try starting a software company and they were supportive. My plan was to take time off, start the company, and then go back later and finish college. I never really made a conscious decision to forgo a degree. Technically, I'm just on a really long leave."

Gates and Allen did not want to use any family money, so they supplied the necessary money to start their new company: Allen invested $606 from his Honeywell job, and Gates provided $910 (largely from poker winnings at late-night Harvard games). Gates received sixty percent ownership because he had done more to develop BASIC, while Allen held the remaining forty percent.

Gates joined Allen in Albuquerque that summer, and the two officially formed their new computer software company. They called it Micro-Soft, a combination of *micro*computer and *soft*ware. Within a few months they changed the company's name to the current version—Microsoft.

Gates and Allen had made an impact on the growing computer industry, but long hours, skill, and a touch of luck would be needed if they hoped to succeed in a big way. Happily, Bill Gates was accustomed to all three.

CHAPTER TWO

A SMART CHILD

Intelligence, decisiveness, and determination coursed through the Gates family tree. Gates's great grandfather on his mother's side, James Willard Maxwell, arrived in Washington State in 1892 and soon established himself as a force in state and local affairs. He became the president and chief stockholder of a bank, and subsequently won election as mayor and served in the state legislature, mainly because he was willing to outwork his competitors. One newspaper article of the day stated that Maxwell always arrived at the bank one hour before the rest of the workers. He moved to the Seattle area shortly before the United States entered World War I in 1917, where he again became part of the city's elite. At the same time, Gates's forebears on his father's side built a thriving furniture-store business in Bremerton.

Gates's father, William H. Gates, II, entered to the legal profession and eventually became a partner in one of Seattle's most prestigious law firms, Shidler McBroom Gates & Lucas. In 1951 he married Mary Maxwell, a teacher with such an impeccable reputation that she was named to the Board of Regents of the University of Washington as well as the boards of many corporations. The couple had three children, two girls—Kristianne, born in 1953, and Libby, in 1962. Their only son, William Henry Gates III, was born in Seattle's Swedish Hospital on October 28, 1955.

WILLIAM HENRY GATES III

Surrounded by a nurturing family that included his grandmother Adelle Maxwell, Gates learned the value of reading and thinking at an early age. The family loved games of every sort, and frequently sat down after dinner to a hotly contested board game or jigsaw puzzle to determine who would have to wash the dishes. His grandmother taught young Bill, whom she called Trey because he was Bill III, to play bridge, a game that demanded strategy and concentration. As his mother recalled in a 1994 biography of her son, "Very early on we played bridge, and she [Grandmother Adelle] was always saying to him, 'Think smart, think smart!'"

William Gates II

By the time he entered school, "thinking smart" was second nature to Bill Gates. His mother said that "He'd never ever be ready when we were going someplace, and we'd call out to him, 'What are you doing?'" Bill usually answered, "I'm thinking, I'm thinking," and then wondered aloud if his parents ever did the same.

His grandmother often read books to Bill and his sisters and, as a result, he developed a love of literature, especially science fiction. He enjoyed an interesting mix of children's classics, such as the Tom Swift series and *Charlotte's Web,* as well as stories by Ray Bradbury and Isaac Asimov. Years later Gates described his childhood in an interview as "a rich environment in which to learn."

Even then, Bill Gates showed flashes of the independent, almost stubborn streak for which he later became famous. Though his mother constantly asked him to clean his perpetually messy room, Bill held out until she agreed to a deal. If he kept the door to his room closed, she would not bother him about what lay behind that wooden separation. The agreement worked to both parties' satisfaction.

Another characteristic that has continued into his adulthood was Bill's habit of rocking back and forth. As a baby he became impatient if someone did not rock his cradle, so he simply started rocking on his own until he fell asleep. At the age of three or four, he rocked back and forth for hours on a rocking horse, smiling happily with the swaying motion. He later explained to a magazine reporter that his love for rocking back and forth while he thinks about major business decisions comes from this childhood habit. "They claim I started at an extremely young age. I had a rocking horse and they used to put me to sleep on my rocking horse, and I think that addicted me."

Little escaped the inquisitive youth's quick

mind. At age nine he visited Seattle's World Fair where, among the marvels, he saw a huge mainframe computer made by IBM (International Business Machines Corporation). His parents openly discussed their work problems with their children and asked them how they might deal with certain issues, hoping to instill responsibility and sound judgment. Bill and his sisters were encouraged to read, rather than watch television,

Gates enjoying a laugh with his sister Libby

and during their school years the television went untouched until the weekend.

Gates loved chatting with his father about the business world. At age eleven, Gates wrote his first contract—a "legal" document—with one of his sisters that allowed him to use her baseball glove. The contract bluntly stated that "When Trey wants the mitt, he gets it." Not only does this incident show his ability to negotiate for what he wanted, but illustrates his ability to convince someone to agree to such a lopsided contract. An older Bill Gates would successfully employ similar tactics in building the Microsoft empire.

FORMAL SCHOOLING BEGINS

By the time he entered View Ridge Elementary School, Gates had a fertile mind that not only absorbed new material, but also questioned its use and practicality. He loved entering reading contests, which he won easily because he read twice as many books as the nearest competitor. Years later he told a magazine writer that "Numbers two through ninety-nine were all girls, and there I was at number one."

The Reverend Dale Turner, the pastor of University Congregational Church, observed an example of Gates's razor-sharp intelligence. Pastor Turner offered a free dinner at Seattle's luxurious Space Needle restaurant to any Sunday-school student who memorized Jesus's Sermon on the Mount. Gates, who attended Turner's Sunday school, quickly mastered the twenty-five-minute sermon and won the dinner. The pastor later recalled, "I needed only to go to his home that day to know that he was something special. I couldn't imagine how an eleven-year-old boy could have a mind like that. And my subsequent questioning of him revealed a deep understanding of the passage."

Up to this point, Gates had never experienced problems with other children. For instance, each summer the family joined other prominent Seattle clans at a camp called Cheerio, where they engaged in a series of games, contests, and fun. Gates relished organizing the activities and competing with the other children.

Once he entered elementary school, however, Gates felt out of place. First of all, his appearance made him a natural target for the other students. Gates buttoned his shirts to the top button and pulled up his pants above his waist, thereby guaranteeing a hostile reception from some students. His high-pitched voice and his small size, along with his natural clumsiness, made the situation worse. "He was a 'nerd' before the term was even invented," said one of his teachers.

Though he loved math and science and did well in those areas, Gates rarely earned high grades in other classes. Bored with the level of the subject matter, Gates misbehaved and goaded classmates into causing trouble. The growing number of requests for parent-teacher conferences alarmed his parents, who knew that their son could do better. Gates's father mentioned that "It wasn't as if he was some kind of obvious super-bright kid. I think we recognize it better looking back than we did at the time. At the time we just thought he was trouble."

His parents faced a tough opponent. Eager to gain his classmates' approval, Gates actually went out of his way to achieve low grades. He later said that "I remember girls always got so much better grades than boys, so it was wimpy to get good grades. So I only got good grades in reading and math. And they always had these things where they'd grade you on your ability and effort, so the goal was always to get an A3, which was the best grade with the worst effort. They'd give me like an A1, and I'd say 'Come on, I didn't try at all.'" Consequently, while Gates earned As in math and science, he compiled Cs and Ds in the subjects he thought were unimportant.

The fact that Gates wanted these low grades

I only got good grades in reading and math.

shows the importance he placed upon being accepted, because he was normally a perfectionist as a student and allowed imperfections nowhere else. His sister, Kristianne, told a biographer that Gates was always trying to improve something. "He was always upset about his little toe curling in, so he'd work on it. He'd spend time holding it out so he'd have a straight toe."

His frustrated parents tried various moves to spark their son's interest. They enrolled Gates in the Boy Scouts and bought the complete *World Book Encyclopedia*, which he read from cover to cover. However, the disruptions and requests for conferences from harried teachers persisted.

Finally, they sent their son to a psychiatrist who, over eighteen months, coaxed Gates into a self-examination and analysis of what was truly important. Though he was doubtful and hesitant at first, Gates gradually saw the value of his visits to the psychiatrist. As he explained in a magazine interview, "[The psychiatrist] said some profound things that got me thinking a little differently. He was a cool guy. . . . I only saw him for a year and a half and never saw him again, and I haven't been to anybody like that since. But my mind was focused appropriately."

As a final step, Bill and Mary Gates took their son out of public school and enrolled him in a nearby private school. His father explained in a recent biography that "We became concerned about him when he was ready for junior high. He was so small and shy, in need of protection, and his interests were so very different from the typical sixth-grader's."

At Lakeside School, Gates would meet another student—a friend with whom he would revolutionize the computer industry.

CHAPTER THREE

GATES DISCOVERS COMPUTERS

In many ways, the Lakeside School differed from Gates's previous experiences. Many of the Seattle area's brightest boys attended grades seven through twelve at Lakeside to prepare them for college. As one student said, "Even the dumb kids [at Lakeside] were smart."

The all-boys school emphasized a unique blend of rules that encouraged the development of individual talents. Faculty and staff expected the boys to work hard, but they also encouraged their students to seek their own voices, to explore areas of special interest, and to begin understanding themselves.

In a book about Bill Gates, one teacher said, "You could, if you looked at Lakeside superficially, think of it as an elitist school with high requirements and strictly focused upon college preparation. But in fact, it tended to look very, very carefully at individual students, especially ones who stuck out in any direction, and it would give those students lots and lots of privilege and rope and space to do whatever they could do, even if it was far out of the usual constraints of the school."

The school's beautiful setting amidst Washington's forested terrain created a tranquil atmosphere on the campus. In some ways, Lakeside provided a secure realm free from the outside world in which the students could pursue their work.

GATES FLOURISHES AT LAKESIDE

Though Gates at first balked at switching schools, he eventually responded to the new challenges in ways that had previously lain dormant. When his parents informed him that he would enter Lakeside, Gates declared that he would purposely fail the entrance exam and thereby squash his parents' strategy. However, Bill and Mary understood their son better than he understood himself. They simply ignored this threat and, as expected, Gates sailed through the entrance examination.

His grades started to improve, although he maintained an overall B average because he still continued to ignore areas that did not interest him. Math held an appeal for Gates, and he eventually enrolled in advanced mathematics classes at the University of Washington while still in high school. Fred Wright, then chairman of the Lakeside Math Department, claimed that Gates "could see shortcuts through an algebraic problem or a computer problem. He could see the simplest way to do things in mathematics."

The avid reader devoured anything he could find on the famous French conqueror, Napoleon Bonaparte, and he impressed teachers with his high intelligence and quick abilities. English teacher Anne S. Stephens remembers handing Gates a three-page script for a school play. He sat down, read the script once, and repeated it word for word. His science teacher, William S. Douglas, said in a magazine interview that "If a teacher was slow, he [Gates] always seemed on the verge of saying, 'But that's obvious.'"

Gates shunned sports at Lakeside to focus on science and mathematical activities. The new world of technology especially fascinated him, and Gates loved to tell students and faculty that he would be a millionaire by his twentieth birthday. He added to what some other students saw as "arrogance" by being selected as a congressional page in Washington, D.C., in the summer between his junior and senior years, and by winning a National Merit Scholarship in his final year.

GATES BECOMES "THE COMPUTER GUY"

While in seventh grade, Gates formed the first close friendship of his life. Kent Evans, the son of a minister, shared Gates's love of mathematics, and before long the two boys were inseparable.

Near the end of their seventh-grade year, a new kind of machine drew their attention. The Lakeside Mothers Club conducted a rummage sale to raise $3,000 so that the school could rent time on a computer. In those days, very few institutions besides large businesses and universities could afford their own computers, but a school could rent time on another institution's computer. The Lakeside Mothers Club figured that $3,000 would rent sufficient time for an entire school year, and, thanks to their fund-raising, Lakeside was one of the first high schools in the United States to have access to the new machines.

They had not bargained on Gates, Evans, and their friends, though. That first year Gates's math teacher, Paul Stocklin, took his class to the computer room for a look at the ASR-33 Teletype, which had a keyboard, a very loud printer, a paper-tape puncher, and a modem. Commands typed on the keyboard were transmitted through telephone lines to a computer owned by General Electric, which performed the requested function. The machine had no screen, and after typing in

Unlike computers today, earlier machines were huge and often hard to operate.

the commands the user would have to wait patiently until the printer clacked out the computer's response. Since Gates was Stocklin's top math student, he allowed Bill to type the first instructions. When the machine printed the proper response, Gates was hooked.

"The computer I was using was huge and cumbersome—and slow and absolutely compelling," Gates later wrote. He and his small circle of friends spent hours with the new device. To

"The computer I was using was huge and cumbersome—and slow and absolutely compelling," play a simple game such as tic-tac-toe, "which would take thirty seconds with a pencil and paper, might consume most of a lunch period. But who cared? There was just something neat about the machine."

Gates quickly mastered that rudimentary computer. His math teacher said, "I knew more [about the computer] than he did for the first day, but only for that first day." Bill Dougall, the teacher assigned to the computer room, added that "It took him a week to pass me [in computer knowledge]." Before long other students referred to Gates as "the computer guy."

Gates never tired of reading about computers, then trying out what he learned by typing instructions in the school's teletype. He became so proficient that he quickly mastered BASIC, a computer's primary language, and designed his own version of tic-tac-toe that could be played on the computer.

Because Gates and Evans spent so much time on the computer, they quickly used up most of the $3,000 raised by the Lakeside Mothers Club. They also tested their teachers' patience, because they handed in almost every non-computer assignment late. Kent Evans's father remembers, "After Lakeside got that computer, Bill and Kent were in constant trouble with the faculty. . . . Everything was late—chemistry workbooks were late, physics workbooks were late, history and English themes were late."

GATES MEETS ALLEN

Gates learned so much about computers that older students at Lakeside came to him for advice. Paul Allen was one student who frequently brought challenges to Gates and dared him to solve the problem by asserting, "Hey, I bet you can't figure this out!"

The two formed a fast friendship and were often spotted together in the hallways or classrooms. While most students warmed to Allen, they kept their distance from the aloof Gates. As one classmate said in a recent biography of Gates, "Paul was cool. He was a nerd who didn't look like a nerd. He was always more approachable and friendlier than Bill. . . . You would run into him in the hallways and he would actually stop and talk to you."

Gates made few close friends. One classmate recalled that Gates "was socially inept and uncomfortable around others. The guy was totally obsessed with his interest in computers. . . . You

Gates watches Paul Allen use the ASR-33 Teletype at the Lakeside School.

would see him playing tennis occasionally, but not much else. Initially, I was in awe of Gates and the others in that [computer] room. I even idolized them to some extent. But I found that they were such turkeys that I didn't want to be like them. . . . They had developed very narrowly socially and they were arrogant, and I just didn't want to be like that. . . ."

Everyone at Lakeside knew that the smartest student there was Bill Gates. And if they forgot, Gates reminded them in irritating ways, such as smirking at what he considered silly answers in class or acting as if some of his teachers were his inferiors. A former classmate mentioned in a biography of Gates that Gates "was obnoxious, he was sure of himself, he was aggressively, intimidatingly smart. When people thought of Bill they thought, well, this guy is going to win a Nobel Prize. But he didn't have any social graces. He just wasn't a personable kind of person. He was one of those guys who knew he was smarter than everyone else and knew he was right all the time. . . ."

Gates, Allen, Kent Evans, and Rick Weiland formed the Lakeside Programmers Group in hopes of using their computer talents to make money. Allen's fascination with the hardware—the computer machine itself—blended perfectly with Gates's love of software—the application programs that give purpose to computers—and they frequently discussed how they could benefit from what they saw as the approaching computer revolution.

One day Gates asked Allen, "Don't you think that someday everybody will have one of these things? And if they did, couldn't you deliver magazines and newspapers and stuff through them?" The two students imagined playing a significant role in the industry and someday earning millions of dollars.

Amazingly, the two actually landed a job while still in school. In 1969, a Seattle-based company called Computer Center Corporation leased a new PDP-10 computer. Since the owner's son attended Lakeside with Gates, the owner offered the boys free computer time if they would test the new computer and remove any bugs, or malfunctions. Gates spent Saturdays and many evenings in downtown Seattle, experimenting with the computer and gaining valuable knowledge. He was so immersed in the project that he frequently crept out of his house at night after his parents went to bed, hopped on a bus, and worked all night at the company's offices. This work eventually led to similar work for other firms.

In 1972, Gates received another assignment. Scheduling classes at Lakeside became vastly more complicated when the school merged with a private girls' school—St. Nicholas. A Lakeside teacher attempted to computerize the schedule, but when he was killed in a plane crash the school asked Gates and Kent Evans to step in. The two practically lived at the school while they wrote a workable program, occasionally sleeping in the teachers' lounge for a few hours rest from their labors.

Another tragedy struck before the project ended, however. In May 1972, Kent Evans was on a mountain hike with some classmates when he lost his footing and fell hundreds of feet to his death. For the next two weeks, a stunned Gates could do little but mourn. When he returned to the scheduling project, Gates asked Paul Allen to help.

The two boys successfully completed the assignment. Gates also managed to create commands in the program that gave him and a select group of friends every Tuesday afternoon free. To celebrate their triumph, which escaped the notice of Lakeside's administrators, the students donned T-shirts bearing the words "Tuesday Club" printed over the outline of a keg of beer.

Gates excluded his friends from one other "change" in the schedule though. For one of his subjects, as he explained in his 1995 book *The Road Ahead*, "I surreptitiously added a few instructions and found myself nearly the only guy in a class full of girls."

GATES AND ALLEN CREATE FIRST COMPANY

Not content to rest on past triumphs, Gates and Allen expanded their loose partnership by forming a company called Traf-O-Data in Gates's senior year. The two developed traffic-counting computers that could analyze traffic flow more quickly, and then attempted to interest cities around the United States. Each time a vehicle passed over a rubber hose stretched across the road, the computer punched its time onto a tape in binary numbers. This permitted city governments to determine which roads required more maintenance or expansion.

While the two students convinced a few cities to try their creation, Traf-O-Data never really caught on. As Allen explained in a magazine article, "Even though Traf-O-Data wasn't a roaring success, it was [important] in preparing us to make Microsoft's first product a couple of years later."

During his senior year, Gates convinced school authorities to grant him a leave so that he

Gates graduates from high school on June 7, 1973.

could work on another project with Paul Allen. The two were asked to computerize the electrical flow at the hydroelectric dams run by a huge government contractor, TRW, near Seattle. Gates convinced Lakeside that his work, for which he would receive $4 per hour, could count as a senior project, and for much of that year he lived in an apartment with Allen while they completed the task. In the spring Gates returned to Lakeside to finish his final year.

In addition to winning the coveted National Merit Scholarship, Gates scored a perfect 800 in math on the Scholastic Aptitude Test (SAT) required of college hopefuls. After eliminating Princeton and Yale as possibilities, Gates entered Harvard University in the fall of 1973.

GATES AT HARVARD UNIVERSITY

Like most college students, Gates found that university life tossed new challenges at him. To his surprise, he learned that he was no longer the brightest mathematics student in the school. Other gifted individuals scored higher marks and made a better impression than Gates, who was flustered by the situation for a time.

He more than made up for it in computer classes, however, where he soon proved that he knew more than the other students—and many of the professors too. The director of Harvard's computer center said that while Gates surpassed everyone intellectually, he was "an obnoxious human being" who taunted fellow students for their slowness.

As was true in high school, Gates worked harder in the classes he enjoyed and scraped by on minimal effort in the others. He related in *The Road Ahead* that he skipped many classes in his freshman year, then mounted a furious charge near semester's end to salvage a decent mark. "It became a game—a not uncommon one—to see how high a grade I could pull while investing the least time possible." Along with his new friend, Steve Ballmer, he ignored class work until a week before final exams, and then studied day and night. Later, Gates admitted that this sort of haphazard preparation, though it worked at Harvard, hadn't been "the best preparation for running a company."

Gates rarely went out on dates, preferring all-night poker games. Ballmer recalls that Gates could play cards until six in the morning, then engage him in a breakfast conversation about some complex mathematical theory as if he had just had a full night's sleep.

Gates kept in contact with Paul Allen, who now worked for Honeywell in the Boston area. The two concluded that since computers would

Steve Ballmer, Gates's friend from Harvard, is now president and CEO of Microsoft.

one day be available for everyone, the public would want the machines to perform a variety of tasks. To do that, software would have to be created to give commands to the computers. At first they assumed they had plenty of time for Gates to complete his college education, but then they saw the January 1975 issue of *Popular Electronics*. The idea of a Harvard degree drifted to the background, completely overshadowed by developments in the fast-paced world of computers.

CHAPTER FOUR

MICROSOFT'S EARLY DAYS

After leaving Harvard in June 1975, Gates joined Allen in Albuquerque, New Mexico, where the two men formed Microsoft. Gates focused his energies started soliciting new clients for their company. He accurately realized that the company's focus should be on operating systems and software applications rather than with hardware, which is the industry lingo for the computer itself. He believed that the production costs for creating hardware would remain relatively high, while systems costs would be comparatively low. If Microsoft got in on the ground floor—before everyone else—it could corner a large share of the market and make big profits.

Gates knew that the operating systems and systems software applications ran hand in hand. As he explained in *The Road Ahead*, "The operating system is a platform on which all the software programs for applications—such as accounting or payroll or word-processing or electronic-mail programs—are built." The two would feed each other, and Microsoft would be there to take advantage.

Gates also foresaw that personal computers would rapidly increase their ability to perform more functions as computer chips improved. Gordon Moore, one of the computer industry's earliest innovators and the co-founder of Intel, stated in what is now known as "Moore's Law" that the number of transistors per chip would double every eighteen months. As the personal computers' capacity to do more increased, software programs would become more important.

This rule meant that a company had a tremendous opportunity for profit, but faced disaster if it allowed the growth to pass it by. Gates intended that Microsoft would take advantage of this rapid growth, and he was even more determined that the company would avoid losing ground by becoming complacent.

GATES HITS THE ROAD

As the market for personal computers expanded, Gates traveled the country to sell Microsoft prod-

Gordon Moore anticipated the rapid growth of computing power in computer chips.

ucts to computer manufacturers, particularly the version of BASIC he had developed for MITS. He became a familiar sight at computer conventions, and his company ran ads in every industry newsletter. He used a simple strategy—offer the product at such a low price that potential customers would not hesitate to buy it. As he mentioned in a recent biography, "We didn't want to give anyone a reason to look elsewhere. We wanted choosing Microsoft software to be a no-brainer." As a company slogan and rallying cry, Gates developed the phrase, "A computer in every home, and Microsoft software on every computer."

> **"A computer in every home, and Microsoft software on every computer."**

Business moved slowly at first. He signed a deal with Commodore International and other firms, but bankruptcies quickly removed most of these customers. Then, in 1977, Gates got his first big break—he signed deals with two of the largest computer manufacturers. Tandy Corporation asked Microsoft to install BASIC into its popular Radio Shack TRS-80 computers, and Apple quickly followed by installing the program on its Apple II computers.

On the heels of these successes, Gates turned his gaze toward Asia. In 1978 he signed a contract with Japanese computer magnate Kazuhiko Nishi, which gave him exclusive distribution rights for BASIC in East Asia. Within one year almost half of Microsoft's business came from Japan.

In spite of these profitable deals, Gates thought

sales of BASIC should be much bigger than they actually were. The numbers of PCs increased daily, but his share of the market did not seem to keep pace. He soon realized that computer users were "pirating" his program—copying Microsoft's software from friends who had earlier purchased it.

In 1976, Gates published an "Open Letter to Hobbyists" in the newsletter *Computer Notes*, explaining that copying software was similar to stealing. He argued that developers of computer software needed to be protected by copyright laws like those that shielded songwriters, and he added that the money lost to pirated versions could have been used in developing improved products. Though the letter did not influence many people at the time—Gates wrote that computer enthusiasts "seemed to like it [BASIC] and used it, but preferred to 'borrow' it from each other."

HECTIC WORKDAYS AT MICROSOFT

In those early years, Microsoft was not the smooth-functioning system that it has since become. Each product and every move appeared to be spontaneous. Everyone in the small firm—fewer than fifteen people—held the common goal of success, but little seemed clearly spelled out. Gates and Allen recruited their first workers from former friends at Harvard and Lakeside, brought them to Albuquerque, and let them sleep on the floor of the apartment Bill shared with Paul Allen.

The workers forged a powerful bond with each other. They were involved in the infancy of a business that had spectacular potential, and they charged into their tasks with zeal. As one member explained, the years in Albuquerque were "almost a missionary kind of work in the sense that we

Microsoft's small group of employees in 1978

were delivering something to [people] they never thought they could have. There was a kinship that you wouldn't normally see in a commercial enterprise."

Gates and Allen shared the decisions and blended well, with Allen producing new ideas and Gates bringing them to reality. Paul Allen said in a magazine interview that "I was probably the one always pushing a little bit in terms of new technology and new products, and Bill was more interested in doing negotiations and contracts and business deals."

As neither of them had previously operated a business, confusion often dominated. The day-to-day concerns were handled as they arose. Gates had not hired a full-time receptionist so whoever was closest answered the telephone or greeted visitors. New employees jumped into the fray with little preparation or assistance, but they were expected to produce immediately. During meetings, everyone gathered around and freely offered his or her opinions. Usually the sessions ended with Gates outshouting his compatriots.

Every worker understood one fact—Gates worked hard, and he demanded that his employees work just as hard as he did. A programmer mentioned that "Bill was always pushing. We would do something I thought was very clever, and he would say, 'Why don't you do this, or why didn't you do that two days ago?' That would get frustrating sometimes."

Gates could be cruel too. Workers became accustomed to hearing their boss shout at someone, "That's the stupidest thing I've ever heard." He wanted to make a profit, not win a popularity contest, and since Gates was the smartest individual in the office, he often exploded at what he considered "inferior" efforts.

Gates boasted about what he called his "seven-hour turnaround." He loved to work at the

Gates and Allen were novices when it came to running a business.

office until late at night, then rush home, eat, get a few hours sleep, and be back in the office within seven hours. He took pride in the feat, but he also realized that if he expected his employees to work hard, he had better push himself more than he goaded them.

GATES OVERCOMES FIRST LEGAL HURDLE

For the first time in his career, Gates faced a legal challenge to his business when the Pertec Computer Corporation sued Microsoft in an effort to halt its sales of BASIC to other companies. Pertec, a huge company, had purchased MITS and believed that it now owned the rights to BASIC. Its executives thought that they would experience little difficulty in shoving aside this newcomer to the market, and when the chief lawyer for Pertec first met Gates, he dismissed the twenty-one-year-old as nothing more than a minor nuisance.

Some people at Microsoft, fearing that the arbitrator—the individual who decides such disputes—would agree with Pertec's arguments, urged Gates to reach a settlement. But Gates, offended by Pertec's high-handed tactics, refused to compromise. At one point, according to a biography written by James Wallace and Jim Erickson, Gates told Paul Allen, "These guys think they've got me over a barrel, but I'm holding my own."

For three weeks, Pertec and Microsoft argued their cases before the arbitrator. If the decision went against Gates, Microsoft might be out of business. However, Pertec's lawyers fell into a ready-made trap. Ed Roberts, former owner of MITS, counseled the lawyers against taking Gates lightly. He recalled that in front of the arbitrator they acted so superior that "it looked like big giant Pertec was picking on these poor nineteen- and twenty-year-old guys and trying to steal their life's work. That's how they [Microsoft] played it and it played pretty well. . . . I told Pertec they needed to deal with Gates hard. But they didn't. It was a fatal mistake. It turns out he won everything."

Even though the legal fees used up much of Microsoft's early profits, Gates remained steadfast. Just as it appeared that Microsoft had depleted its financial resources—Gates's parents had even offered money to their son—the arbitrator ruled in Microsoft's favor. The company retained the rights to BASIC and could now look forward to unimpeded sales of the program.

GATES HEADS TO SEATTLE

Near the end of 1978, Gates and Allen decided to move company headquarters out of Albuquerque. Their recent legal battle with Pertec had left them little incentive to remain in New Mexico, and Gates found it hard to persuade workers to join him in the desert when they could accept offers elsewhere.

At first Gates and Allen considered moving to Silicon Valley near San Francisco where many other computer companies had settled. However, they feared that having their rivals in such close proximity might lure Microsoft's workers away. Besides, California's high cost of living meant that they would have to raise their employees' salaries. Finally, Gates hoped to establish a unique identity for Microsoft, and he decided that goal could better be accomplished away from other computer concerns.

He and Allen selected the state of Washington. They would not have to pay spiraling salaries in the Northwest with its lower cost of living, and locating near Seattle would place them back amid family and friends. In late 1978 twelve of Microsoft's employees moved with Gates and Allen to their new offices on the eighth floor of a commercial building in Bellevue, Washington, directly across Lake Washington from Seattle.

One of Gates's first moves in Washington was to hire someone who could run the company more efficiently. Up to this point, Gates participated in hiring people, setting their wages, and defining their responsibilities. However, as Microsoft expanded, Gates would need to focus on the most crucial decisions.

For assistance, Gates turned to his Harvard classmate and friend Steve Ballmer. A determined businessman with a stubbornness to match that of Gates, Ballmer quickly clashed with Gates over hiring additional personnel. Ballmer wanted to add fifty new workers, but Gates refused to allow such an expansion. As he wrote in *The Road Ahead*, "I wanted Microsoft to be lean and hungry."

The two engaged in a titanic battle, but no matter how angry Gates became, Ballmer insisted the company needed the workers. Finally, Ballmer's persistence won the day. Gates told him to "Just keep hiring smart people as fast as you can, and I will tell you when you get ahead of what we can afford."

Ballmer's stance proved correct. The intelligent people he hired formed Microsoft's backbone as it rushed through the coming computer revolution. They created new products, explored ways to develop others, and spearheaded the company's amazing explosion in the 1980s and 1990s. Microsoft's profits constantly grew over those decades, so Gates never had to tell his friend to slow the pace of hiring.

CHAPTER FIVE

GATES BECOMES A SOFTWARE GIANT

In mid-1980 Microsoft started its swift rise to dominance in the computer industry. The commercial giant, IBM, which had focused on making the huge mainframe computers used by large businesses, wanted to enter the personal computer (PC) market. Since they trailed companies such as Apple, which had already started in this field, IBM executives wanted to place a product on store shelves as soon as possible. They decided to buy software and other necessary parts they needed instead of developing them on their own. For this purpose, they turned to Bill Gates.

AN ALLIANCE WITH IBM

In July, IBM executives asked Gates and Allen to create both a computer language for their upcoming PC, like the one they had completed for MITS, and an operating system. In effect, IBM would create the machine, and they wanted Gates and Allen to produce the engine for the revolutionary device. Because of other contractual commitments, Gates and his partner were not sure they could meet IBM's deadline of one year, so they recommended that IBM talk to another firm

IBM was not able to close a deal with the second business and they returned to Microsoft. Gates knew that a successful union with a company as profitable as IBM could secure Microsoft's future, but only if he could develop a workable product within one year—and that was far from a guarantee. In the meantime, he would have to commit a sizable amount of Microsoft's money, time, and resources. If something went wrong, he would jeopardize Microsoft's future. Gates discussed the issue with Allen and other trusted executives and then decided they had no choice but to accept the deal. He was taking a huge risk, but he felt that the potential benefits outweighed the risk. Gates turned to his fellow workers and firmly stated, "Gotta do it."

Gates turned to his fellow workers and firmly stated, "Gotta do it."

Gates flew to Florida to meet with IBM executives, who were startled to see such a young-

Other businessmen often underestimated Gates because of his youthful appearance.

looking man enter their conference room. Some wondered if he might be an office boy. When they realized who he was, they quietly smirked at the prospect of facing such an untested rookie. One executive recalled that IBM thought Gates was a "hacker" or "a harmless nerd." But they soon learned that they were meeting with a man who "has been bred for the accumulation of great power and maximum profit, the child of a lawyer, who knew the language of contracts, and who just ripped those IBM guys apart."

The IBM people quickly changed their attitudes. Gates's command of computer knowledge impressed every person in the room, and the speed and clarity with which he presented his facts left no doubt that this was a gifted individual. "He was obviously in control," said one of the IBM executives. "He's one of the smartest men I've ever known."

In November 1980, Gates and IBM finalized the arrangement in which Microsoft agreed to develop the operating system and software for IBM. According to the terms, kept secret so that competitors would not learn about the new product until shortly before its unveiling, for each PC sold by IBM, Microsoft would receive a payment for the operating system and the software. Gates astutely retained the rights to sell the same programs to other PC producers, which meant that

Microsoft could earn profits from machines manufactured by just about every company entering the field.

This deal showed that when Gates joined with other companies, the tough bargainer negotiated contracts that tilted heavily in Microsoft's favor. As his friend and fellow industrialist Warren Buffett said, "If Bill had started a hot dog stand, he would have become the hot dog king of the world. He will win in any game."

INTRODUCING MS-DOS

Gates returned to Washington and immediately put his team to work on the project. With a one-year deadline, Gates knew he could not waste a single moment. Allen said that they might save weeks of effort if they could purchase an operating system from some other company and then adapt it to the IBM PC. However, Microsoft could not let the other company know why they needed an operating system or that company would simply go to IBM and make its own deal. Allen added that a local firm called Seattle Computer had a system they might purchase.

Two days after combining with IBM, Gates bought Seattle Computer for $50,000. Because the arrangement provided Microsoft with an operating system and helped cement the pact with IBM,

Gates's purchase has been labeled the "deal of the century" by industry analysts. When executives at Seattle Computer later learned of IBM's involvement, however, they accused Gates of cheating them out of potential profits. This would not be the last time someone criticized Gates for what they thought were unfair, ruthless tactics.

For the next year, Gates and Allen struggled to perfect the systems. Everyone involved was sworn to secrecy, and IBM even sent unannounced inspectors to Microsoft headquarters to check that they carefully guarded the two prototype PCs. Finally, in mid-1981, they completed MS-DOS (Microsoft Disk Operating System), allowing IBM to introduce its PC on August 12, 1981.

Computer enthusiasts loved the new machine and rushed to purchase it. To compete, other companies made similar versions of the IBM personal computers—"clones" as they were called in the business. But, since the other computer makers did not know how to duplicate Gates's MS-DOS, they had to purchase Microsoft products for their PCs. Gates and Allen sat back and watched as money poured in on every PC sold, whether IBM or a competing brand. In 1981, Microsoft's profit jumped from $4 million to $16 million, and one observer claimed that Gates and Allen "create[d] more wealth than any business partners in the history of American commerce." IBM executives,

Gates and Allen in early days of Microsoft

worried that other companies were eating into its market share with their own PCs, condemned Gates as a traitor for selling operating systems to those companies as well.

Though Microsoft's financial future appeared set with the IBM contract, conditions at the company drastically changed within one year. On a business trip to Europe, Paul Allen suddenly felt weakened. "One day in Paris," he mentioned in a magazine interview, "I just felt really bad and decided I had to go back to the States." Physicians diagnosed Allen as suffering from Hodgkin's disease, a form of cancer with a relatively high cure rate.

Three months of radiation therapy removed Allen from the day-to-day events at Microsoft and gave him time to reflect upon his life. "To be thirty years old and have that kind of shock—to face your mortality—really makes you feel like you should do some of the things that you haven't done."

Following the radiation treatments, Allen's doctors told him that if the cancer did not reappear within two years, he could consider himself cured. Allen took a lengthy leave to spend time with family, travel, and restore his health, and then, instead of returning to the frantic pace at Microsoft, he decided to retire. Doctors eventually declared Allen cured, and he subsequently rejoined the industry on a limited basis by starting his own software company.

MICROSOFT GOES PUBLIC

In August 1985, Microsoft celebrated its tenth anniversary. From its humble origins, the company had grown to more than 1,000 employees and enjoyed annual sales approaching $200 million. That summer Gates started construction of new corporate headquarters on 270 acres (109 hectares)

The Microsoft campus in 1986

of forested land near Redmond, Washington. Called the Corporate Campus because it looked like a university setting, the new headquarters consisted of twenty-six buildings constructed around a huge pond, known as "Lake Bill."

The next year, Gates became a thirty-one-year-old billionaire—the youngest American to achieve that pinnacle—when Microsoft offered shares in the company to the public. As the stock's value rapidly multiplied, Gates, who held the largest number of shares, saw his net worth rise accordingly. To celebrate, Gates took a rare four-day sailing vacation off Australia.

COMPETITION WITH APPLE

Gates's main competition in the 1980s came from Apple Computer and its magnetic co-founders, Steve Jobs and Steve Wozniak, who constructed a user-friendly computer that appealed to educational institutions and publishing firms. The main attraction was its simple operating system. Rather than requiring a series of typed instructions to open a program, like Microsoft's DOS, the Apple operating system simply required the user to move an arrow to an icon (picture) and click the handheld mouse. Customers loved the eye-catching graphics that appeared on-screen, such as an image of a file or a wastebasket, and the ease with

Executives from Apple Computer—Steve Jobs, chairman, John Scully, president and chief operating officer, and Steve Wozniak, co-founder—unveil a new Apple computer in 1984.

which they could move from program to program. The graphical user interface (GUI), as it was called, brought numerous customers to Apple.

When Apple introduced its Macintosh computer in 1981, the company did not control a large share of the market and its computer was not compatible with IBM machines. However, Gates worried that Microsoft would lose customers to Apple's simpler operating system. So, instead of ignoring Apple, like many other companies did, Gates signed a contract with Jobs and Wozniak in 1982 to develop programs that could run on the Macintosh. Simultaneously, he ordered company researchers to develop a GUI that could be operated on IBM-compatible machines. This meant he could make a profit with both Apple *and* IBM machines.

Gates had to walk a perilous road. He could not offend IBM, with whom he was collaborating on a third version of an operating system labeled OS/2, nor could he offend Apple, for whom he produced software programs. He also faced a problem in that IBM computers did not have enough memory to run a GUI. However, he pushed his programmers to perfect a competing system for Microsoft so that when their computer capacity increased, they could immediately start selling it.

To keep potential customers from buying Apple computers, Microsoft announced its first graphics operating system—Windows—in 1983, even though the product was far from complete. By announcing programs before they were ready—"vaporware"—Gates discouraged customers from buying a rival product before his product was on the market.

Microsoft introduced Windows 1.0 in 1985 to negative reviews. Because Gates had hurried his programmers, the new program had many bugs, or problems, and the complex program used up most of an IBM-compatible computer's memory. Worried Microsoft executives advised Gates to drop the program and concentrate on application software, but Gates plowed ahead. If Moore's Law was valid—and hardware capacity doubled every eighteen months—computers would soon carry enough memory for Windows. In the meantime, he ordered his developers to remove every imperfection from Windows.

His plan worked. In 1988, Microsoft introduced Windows 2.0, followed two years later by Windows 3.0, a vastly improved GUI that stunned executives at Apple and IBM. Apple worried because now an IBM-compatible PC could be operated as simply as a Macintosh, and IBM executives saw their much-heralded OS/2 program, co-developed with Gates, overshadowed by Gates's better system.

Because of the success of Windows, Microsoft became the largest software company in the world. Again, Gates made enemies with what competitors saw as double-dealing and back-stab-

No matter what anyone said, Gates believed that the Windows operating system would succeed.

bing. IBM claimed that Gates put only a token effort into their combined OS/2 program so that his Windows would gain a larger share of the market, and Apple said he had copied their graphics. As a result, Microsoft and IBM turned into bitter enemies.

In March 1988, Apple sued Microsoft for illegally copying aspects of its operating system. After a protracted five-year dispute, a judge dismissed the case and permitted Microsoft to continue marketing Windows.

GATES BUILDS HIS COMPANY

With the incredible developments at Microsoft, Gates stood on the verge of a rapid expansion. Besides operating systems, Microsoft moved into word processing systems, financial planning programs, and spreadsheets. In an effort to widen its market, Microsoft shared information about its products with other software companies so that they would develop programs compatible with MS-DOS. Before long, Microsoft cornered seventy-three percent of the spreadsheet market and seventy-three percent of the word processing market.

One can see the hand of Bill Gates in every move made at Microsoft. *People* magazine described Gates as "part innovator, part entre-

*Gates relies on Ballmer to help to keep
Microsoft running smoothly.*

preneur, part salesman, and full-time genius."
The astute businessman has incorporated practices designed to improve productivity and effi-
ciency, and he has maintained a relentless
vigilance against complacency. Since Gates wanted his company to stay lean and frugal, one of

Steve Ballmer's main responsibilities was to guard against overspending. As Ballmer explained to *The New Yorker* magazine, "If you're going to work for this company, you're going to rent a certain kind of car and stay in a certain kind of hotel and fly coach, because that's business, and anything else is just [luxury]." The one time that Bill Gates chartered a private airplane rather than taking a commercial airplane flight, Ballmer chewed him out for wasting company money.

To keep a small-business atmosphere at Microsoft, Gates breaks his divisions into groups of no more than two hundred employees. He hopes to maintain a team approach in this manner so that every worker feels he or she is both contributing to Microsoft's success and held accountable for any failures.

Though the company had expanded its employee count to keep pace with business, Gates wants as small a workforce as possible. As he said to *Fortune* magazine, "Once you allow managers to think it takes one hundred people to do something when it should be twenty, that's extremely hard to reverse." As a result, he intentionally does not hire as many people as needed and takes pride that Microsoft employs fewer programmers than its competitors.

The company's amazing success, however, makes it necessary to hire a substantial number of workers each year simply to keep pace with growth. To make sure he receives a steady stream of top-notch talent, Gates has established a recruiting network throughout the best colleges. In 1991, company recruiters examined 120,000 résumés, interviewed 7,400 people, and hired only 2,000. While offering lower salaries than his competitors, Gates attracts the best minds by giving them large amounts of responsibility right away and by offering them shares in Microsoft.

In return Gates demands hard work. At Microsoft, 60- to 80-hour workweeks are the norm—a backbreaking schedule unless compared to that of Gates, who consistently arrives at the office no later than 8:00 A.M. and remains until near midnight. On Sundays, his only day off, Gates usually spends two to three hours reading memos or electronic mail (e-mail).

A UNIQUE WORKPLACE

Gates enjoys an unusual degree of loyalty not found at most companies by giving his workers a great deal of freedom to perform their tasks. Rather than trying to follow a long list of stultifying rules and a dress code, workers set their own hours, perform tasks in their own way, and unless they are hosting a visiting group, they can dress

*While Gates's employees work hard, they do
have a few moments for fun.*

as they please. Some arrive in sweat suits and
running shoes; others wear suits and ties.

Steve Ballmer remembers an IBM executive
telling him what he observed when watching one
of Microsoft's programmers. When Ballmer
inquired who the programmer was, the IBM visitor could not remember the man's name. Instead
he referred to him as "the guy without shoes."

Free memberships to health clubs, espresso
stations dispensing free coffee in each building,

Gates follows the company's casual style himself.

frequent parties, and annual picnics lighten the workload. A visitor to the Redmond campus is as likely to see a group of youthful-looking engineers or programmers in T-shirts and jeans battling on one of the corporate softball diamonds as to catch them in a conference room.

Employees who cannot handle either the excessive demands or the casual working style are asked to either leave the company or accept another job within Microsoft. A less than a six percent turnover rate attests to the success of Microsoft's system, along with the presence of wealth, of course. Microsoft has more millionaire workers than any other company in the world.

Bill Gates personifies the "look" at Microsoft by dressing casually and by frequently using contemporary terms, such as "cool," "neat," "super," and "supercool," to describe people or ideas he likes. A 1985 *Rolling Stone* profile depicted him as "an undernourished graduate student, given to sweaters, corduroys and a certain adolescent awkwardness." However, his looks belie the talents and the ferocious nature underneath. One of Gates's co-workers told *The New Yorker* magazine that at Microsoft, "There are probably more smart people per square foot here than anywhere else in the world, but Bill is just smarter."

Workers get an up-close glimpse of Gates in a series of dreaded "Bill meetings." A reporter for *Business Week* wrote that "Employees speak knowingly of 'Bill meetings,' which sound only slightly better than the Spanish inquisition. Gates peppers his workers with technical questions. He challenges, he makes judgments, he finds flaws—whether in a faulty algorithm or a poorly-targeted marketing plan. Employees have been known to crib for weeks, even holding practice meetings, for one sixty-minute session with Gates."

Should a worker falter under his scrutiny, Gates—constantly rocking in his chair at a pace that quickens as the tension increases—intensifies the examination. An executive who has endured such ordeals says "You have to be able to take this abuse and fight back. If you back down, he loses respect. It's part of the game."

Besides meetings, Gates communicates with his workers through e-mail. Most working days, he spends two hours reading and writing e-mail, and so do his employees. Instead of relying on the telephone, workers at Microsoft send 200 million e-mails every month.

CHAPTER SIX

LIFE OUTSIDE THE OFFICE

For years, Gates worked hard to ensure Microsoft's success, often at the risk of neglecting his personal life. Gates dated a number of women through the 1980s, but most could not tolerate his hectic work schedule. Rather than accommodate their lives to the demands of Microsoft, most simply drifted in and out of his life. Ann Winblad, a successful computer consultant from Chicago, understood Gates's arduous lifestyle and dated him for several years.

Though he has improved in recent times, his poor hygiene and sense of fashion were legendary for years. Ann Winblad explained that "A lot of friends have said, 'Bill, come on, let's go on a shopping spree, we'll buy you some clothes,' but it never works. Bill just doesn't think about clothes. And his hygiene is not good. And his glasses—how can he see out of them? But Bill's attitude is: I'm in this pure mind state, and clothes and hygiene are last on the list."

Gates left little time for relaxation as well. From 1978 to 1984, he missed only six days of work, and the few vacations he took usually involved reading books on a beach and eating canned tomato soup or SpaghettiOs. In 1987, he vacationed in Brazil with Ann Winblad and both spent the days lounging on beaches engrossed in a pile of books about biology. As Winblad explained, "You see, to Bill, life is school. There's always something more to learn."

Winblad helped Gates handle the mounting social obligations imposed by his position at Microsoft. Shy in large gatherings, Gates hated being the center of attention, so Winblad found that she had to help bring him into conversations. She explained to *The New Yorker* magazine that it was not so much that Gates did not want to chat with people, but that "he doesn't have the social skills to do it on his own. But that doesn't mean he isn't social. Bill is an open, emotional guy—very. He's actually more open with his feelings than most men I know. He is not afraid to express fear, or sadness, but hardly anyone sees that. You can't show that when you're in Bill's position, when everyone is watching your tiniest gesture. It's not good leadership to show weakness."

Gates is so consumed with his work at Microsoft that he sometimes lacks knowledge most people would readily possess. For instance, the famous singer and musician, Sting, once asked to visit with Gates. Before meeting with the singer, Gates had to ask a friend who the man was. Following their conversation, however, Gates paid Sting one of the highest compliments he can give when he told an associate Sting was "a really smart guy."

GATES SETTLES DOWN

In 1988, a year after Gates and Winblad ended their relationship, Gates met Melinda French, a Microsoft manager nine years younger than himself. The two conducted an on-again, off-again relationship over the next five years—they even broke up for almost a year at one point—which drove Gates's mother crazy. Anxious to see her famous son settle down, Mary Gates kept asking when he would propose to Melinda.

In March 1993, he finally asked her. In a storybook tale that few people other than Gates could afford, he chartered a jet for the two of them on the pretense that they were going on a brief Sunday trip, then in midair had the aircraft diverted to Omaha, Nebraska while the perplexed French

Gates's relationship with Melinda had many ups and downs before they became engaged.

wondered what was going on. Still in the dark about the day's events, French followed Gates to a waiting limousine which transported the couple to Borsheim's, a famous jewelry store owned by Gates's close friend, Warren Buffett. The store had been opened that Sunday exclusively for Gates and French. He asked Melinda to marry him, then led her inside so that she—the sole customer in the store—could select a ring.

The size of the ring reflected Gates's wealth. Buffett told Gates that when he had asked his wife to marry him, he spent six percent of his net worth on a ring as a symbol of commitment. He urged Gates to do the same for Melinda.

News of Gates's engagement pleased not only family and friends, but also competitors in the computer industry who had bristled at occupying second-place to Gates and Microsoft. With family obligations, they hoped Gates would slow down. As one rival vice president commented, partly in jest, "If the rest of the industry is lucky, he'll have a couple of kids soon."

On January 1, 1994, with close friend and associate Steve Ballmer as best man, Gates wed Melinda French in a lavish million-dollar ceremony on the Hawaiian island of Lanai. To protect the couple, their families, and the 130 wedding guests from reporters and photographers, Gates rented

Gates's wedding ceremony in Lanai, Hawaii,
on January 1, 1994

every car and hotel room on the island. As added
security, everyone working on the wedding had to
sign a nondisclosure statement, and the press was
given an inaccurate date for the ceremony.

A FAMILY MAN

Two years later, in April 1996, Melinda gave birth
to their first child, Jennifer. While Gates appears

to thrive on being a husband and parent—in 1998 he appeared on the television show "20/20" and sang Jennifer's favorite song, "Twinkle Twinkle Little Star"—he has not slowed his business schedule in any manner.

On May 23, 1999, the couple's second child, son Rory John Gates, was born in Seattle. The 8-pound, 11-ounce (3.6 kg) boy gave Gates and Melinda more reason to focus on home, and though Gates makes a conscious effort to do so, the burdens of running an immense corporation keep him at his work for long hours.

In 1997, Bill, Melinda, and Jennifer moved into their new home, which stands on the shore of Lake Washington. It is an immense 40,000-square-foot (3,700 square-meters) compound (about twenty times the size of the average American residence). It consists of five houses, a twenty-car garage, and a house for a caretaker. Gates installed the most recent technology in this dream setup, including computer-controlled locks, lighting systems, music system, and video walls that can project any of countless digital reproductions of famous artistic masterpieces. The residence also has a 14,000-book library, a dining area that seats 100, a racquetball court, a swimming pool with an underwater stereo system, and a trout stream.

In spite of the obvious trappings of wealth,

rather than acting as royalty Gates considers himself an average person who loves to eat pizza and hamburgers with his family. He tries to shield his family from people who might try to take

An aerial view of Gates's house on Lake Washington

advantage of his wealth, and he guards against raising his children to look down on others.

Each Fourth of July, he stages a huge theme party for more than one hundred family members and friends. One year he had six tons of sand trucked in for a huge sand-castle contest. Another year he decided on a western theme and brought in country singer-songwriter Kris Kristofferson for entertainment.

LEARNING TO RELAX

By small stages, Gates has brought relaxation into his life, though certainly not to the degree that most people have. He is now an avid golfer and even appeared in a Callaway golf commercial, and he tries to fit in a few pleasure trips. In October 1995 he took Melinda, Jennifer, his father, and Warren Buffett to China to celebrate his fortieth birthday.

A voracious reader, Gates devours biographies so that he can study how great persons in history solved problems. As he told *Fortune* magazine, "I am always fascinated by the question of whether the most talented people end up in critical positions—in

It's amazing the way some people develop during their lives.

*Gates takes time out of his hectic
schedule to play golf.*

politics, business, academia, or the military. It's amazing the way some people develop during their lives." When he does not read for relaxation, he enjoys watching videotapes of Nobel Prize-winning physicist Richard Feynman's physics lectures.

Gates has also cultivated a serious interest in antiques. In 1994, he paid $30.8 million for the Codex Hammer, the seventy-two-page notebook containing Leonardo da Vinci's writings and drawings on different topics from 1506 to 1510. He also founded Corbis, a company that will place thousands of the world's artistic masterpieces into a digital archive, which will be available to consumers through computers. As part of this, he acquired the Bettmann Archive, a collection of 16 million historic photographs and images.

TIME TO GIVE BACK

While Gates may use his wealth to acquire luxuries and provide for his family, he has begun in recent years to give sizable donations to charitable causes. In 1998, he and Melinda announced that they were donating $20 million to Duke University, Melinda's alma mater, to provide financial assistance for undergraduates. They have also

Bill and Melinda Gates announce their donation to the children's vaccine program in New York in 1998.

pledged $12 million to the University of Washington for bioengineering research, $6 million to Stanford University for a computer science center, and earmarked $1 million each year for United Way charities.

CHAPTER SEVEN

GATES FACES NEW CHALLENGES

In the early 1990s, Gates was at the top of the world, both personally and professionally. He was successful at continuing to build Microsoft's business. Much of the company's expansion came through improving existing products, such as Windows, and by entering new areas, particularly in cable television and the information superhighway. His success reaped huge financial dividends for shareholders. An investor who purchased 100 shares of Microsoft stock in 1986 paid $2,100; by 1993 the same shares had skyrocketed in value to $77,850. Microsoft earned twice as much as Apple and outsold its three largest competitors combined. In the early 1990s, when rival firms experienced financial setbacks and had to let some of their young executives go, Microsoft had the money to snap them up.

Despite Microsoft's strong position in the

computer world, Gates pushed his employees to work harder than ever and warned them that nothing could be taken for granted in the fast-paced world of computers, where new products arrive one day and are replaced by an improved version the next. As he mentioned to a magazine reporter, "In this busi-

Unless you're running scared all the time, you're gone.

ness, by the time you realize you're in trouble, it's too late to save yourself. Unless you're running scared all the time, you're gone."

An example of this is the 1999 publication of Gates's second book, *Business @ the Speed of Thought*, in which he argued that companies must remain on top of the heady changes that constantly alter the business world. In his book, he promoted what he called the Digital Nervous System, a computer/Internet-centered network that produces information in split seconds. He contended that businesses that do not adapt to a speedy information system will lag behind those that do.

Gates surrounded himself with high-energy executives who labored long into the night to ensure Microsoft did not falter. Steve Jobs told *Fortune* magazine that "Bill has done a great job of cloning himself as the company has grown. Now

*Gates with business school students at a
book-signing event in London*

there are all these aggressive 'Little Bills' running
the various product groups and divisions, and
they keep coming at you and coming at you and
coming at you . . . They're not afraid to stumble,
and they have all this money so they can afford to
hire anybody they want. So now they can *really*
keep coming at you."

Gates closed a string of deals. In 1994, to take

advantage of the profitable educational field, he merged with one of the leading educational publishers, Scholastic Corporation, to develop products for the growing youth market. Believing that in the future most financial transactions will be done through computer transfers of funds, in 1995 he moved Microsoft into the world of banking by forging an alliance with Chemical Bank. The next year he vaulted into the cable industry in a partnership with the National Broadcasting Company (NBC) to produce CD-ROM software, online news services, and television programs. That year the two companies launched MS-NBC, a 24-hour news and business cable channel.

CRITICISM OF MICROSOFT GROWS

Success comes with a price, though, and Gates has invariably made enemies of rival business leaders who feel he has either bullied his way into a deal or has acted in some unfair manner. Consequently, criticism of Gates and Microsoft, never much of a factor in the company's early days, reached fever pitch in the 1990s. Some complained that Microsoft has created a monopoly— total control of a market—in the computer industry by owning both an operating system (Windows) and application programs.

For instance, when Windows 95 and its

accompanying Internet browser—a program that permits the computer user to log onto the Internet—appeared in the middle of the decade, cable companies offering access to the Internet complained that Microsoft unfairly excluded them from the market. They believed that the purchaser of a computer should have a choice of options for gaining access to the Internet rather than the only one—Microsoft's—offered by Windows 95.

Hostility toward Microsoft and Gates has taken on gigantic, and sometimes bizarre, dimensions. People have created websites on the Internet that are dedicated to poking fun at him and his company. During a 1998 business trip to Belgium, as Gates walked to a meeting, a prankster dashed out of the crowd and smacked him in the face with a cream pie.

Gates realizes that some of this hostility comes from jealousy, but he has had to spend an alarming amount of time fending off attacks. Rival companies have not only logged numerous complaints with the federal government about unfair business practices, but they have aided government investigations by supplying information in hopes of stunting Microsoft's growth. Executives from Apple, Intel, and other companies have testified about what they view as Microsoft's bullying tactics. One source told *Time* magazine, "We knew whom to direct Justice to at IBM, Compaq, and Gateway, because we'd all shared beers at computer conferences together. After a long day, we'd sit around and complain about Microsoft."

One competing executive told *The New Yorker* magazine, "Hey—I think the guy [Gates] is truly dangerous. Bill is the most surprisingly conscience-free individual I've ever met, and that amount of power in the hands of a guy without a conscience is dangerous."

Gates's rivals fear that Microsoft has achieved such a strong monopoly on the market that he will stifle competition. Currently, Microsoft commands close to ninety percent of the operating systems in the world PC market and almost half of the software market, leaving little room for would-be competitors. Those companies claim that such dominance by one firm is not in the best interests of the consumer.

Gates has a ready answer for these critics. "Our success is based on only one thing: good products. It's not very complicated. We're not powerful enough to cause products that are not excellent to sell well."

IS MICROSOFT A MONOPOLY?

As early as 1991, the Federal Trade Commission (FTC) began examining Microsoft's practices to

*Many of Gates's competitors have been
concerned by his company's leading position
on the software market.*

determine if any abuse had occurred. Two years
later the FTC closed its investigation without fil-
ing charges, but antitrust investigators from the
Department of Justice (DOJ) stepped in. Government action heated up in 1997 when Microsoft
introduced its Internet browser, Internet Explorer
4.0, as part of its Windows operating system.
Other companies, particularly Netscape with its

Navigator browser, instantly complained that Gates had again tried to dominate both the computer and the Internet markets.

The DOJ's antitrust chief, Joel Klein, said that Microsoft had violated the United States's Sherman Act, which bans a company from using a monopoly in one branch of industry to force its way into a second branch. Klein claimed that Microsoft violated this act by combining (bundling) its Internet browser, Explorer, with Windows and selling it as one piece.

Klein worried that Microsoft would control the public's access to the Internet and its upcoming "information superhighway." Explaining the government's position, Klein said, "Microsoft has taken two separate products—the operating system and the browser—and illegally tied them together. In order to make sure this market doesn't tip and become a monopoly, we thought the most effective, immediate relief would be to ensure carriage for Netscape as the only company that can prevent monopolization." In other words, he wanted Microsoft to either ship Windows without the browser or to offer both its own Explorer, as well as their competitor's Navigator, on their Windows operating systems.

Klein believed that the government's position reflected what was best for the nation. "Mr. Gates has in mind Microsoft innovation. I have in mind all the innovation that all the great software companies of America can bring to market. We are telling all these companies, put your heart and the sweat of your brow into making new and great products, and we will make sure you get a chance to compete." To support his position, Klein has even used some of the e-mails that passed from one Microsoft executive to another, stating that to gain an upper hand on Netscape they had better tie in their own browser with Windows. They mentioned that if a customer starts a computer that automatically offers Microsoft's browser, they will use it without thinking. As one Microsoft executive allegedly said, "We are going to cut off [Netscape's] air supply. Everything they're selling, we're going to give away for free."

MICROSOFT DEFENDS ITSELF

Microsoft countered these objections by stating that removing Explorer from Windows would require lengthy—and costly—rewrites of the elaborate operating system code, which contains 18.2 million lines. The other government suggestion, to include Navigator as well as Explorer, rankled Microsoft executives. As one said, "It would be a lot like asking Coca-Cola to ship three Pepsis with every six-pack."

Gates asserted that rather than helping the

*Gates speaks to a judiciary committee
on March 3, 1993.*

consumer, the government was actually "trying to [give an] advantage [to] a competitor of ours. That's really unprecedented. Netscape was able to get the government working on its behalf." A computer consultant told *Fortune* magazine that "The sad thing now is that some of these companies [who want to halt Microsoft] think of the Department of Justice as their best competitive weapon to use against Microsoft." Gates wondered how Klein could argue that Microsoft hurt the consumer when Microsoft has made the personal computer both a better product and more affordable.

Gates claimed that consumers support Microsoft because they want an easy-to-use product, and an integrated item such as Windows with a browser achieves that goal. "When we talk to consumers and to computer manufacturers, they ask us to make the system simpler. That requires more integration. Preventing us from doing that would be a step backward."

Gates, who explained that "In its heyday, IBM was never loved," stated that the future holds opportunity for everyone. New areas will emerge that any enterprising entrepreneur can exploit, new alliances will propel fresh companies to the top, and improved products will test the strengths of existing ones. The computer industry contains such vast areas of unexplored territory, according to Gates, that one company will never be able to dominate the market.

Joseph Guglielmi, the chief executive officer of Taligent, a joint Apple-IBM project to develop a new operating system to rival Microsoft, agreed with Gates. "Today, everyone is in fear of Microsoft. But in the end, everyone will compete. There are thousands of Bill Gateses out there who will find pieces of this market and win them."

TRYING TO FIND A SOLUTION

As the government pursued its case against Microsoft, a number of possible solutions emerged. Klein could recommend that Microsoft be allowed to retain its two main components—operating system and software applications—but require them to operate independently from each other. He could also try to split Microsoft into separate companies, one producing the operating system and the other focusing on software applications, just as the government earlier broke the huge telephone conglomerate, AT&T, into smaller units.

Danger exists in any course of action. Microsoft built its empire through innovative practices, but in spending so much time and resources defending itself in court against the DOJ, the company might lose its competitive edge. That could harm the entire industry. As a reporter for *Time* magazine wrote, "Bill Gates could find himself fending off Justice in perpetuity [forever], a prospect which in turn raises the fear that the company could come to resemble the IBM that emerged from thirteen years of tortuous antitrust wars a wounded giant—drained of the competitive fire that helped spark the computer revolution."

If the government adopts the harsh step of asking a court to split Microsoft apart, some observers wonder if Gates would simply move the firm out of Seattle into neighboring Canada, which does not have strict anti-trust laws. A writer for *Time* magazine even suggested Gates might take a more aggressive step. People in the industry discussed that "Gates could buy a Caribbean island and take Microsoft offshore. On the Isle of Gates, every computer would run Windows, and there would be no such thing as antitrust law."

In October 1997, the Department of Justice sued Microsoft for forcing computer makers to use Explorer if they want to include Windows 95 on their product. When, two months later, Judge Thomas Penfield Jackson issued a preliminary injunction ordering Microsoft to sell Windows without its browser, Microsoft lawyers appealed the decision. The following May a federal appeals court ruled that Jackson's injunction applied to Windows 95, but not to its updated version due to appear on the market, Windows 98.

In response, on May 14, 1998, the Department of Justice, in conjunction with twenty state attorneys general, sued Microsoft for antitrust violations. The DOJ and Microsoft have remained locked in a courtroom battle that has captured the attention of every computer company. Despite the ongoing legal maneuvers, Microsoft still enjoys a high level of consumer confidence. Since the trial's start, the value of a Microsoft share has risen thirty-three percent. As a *Time* magazine reporter concluded, "Somewhere, Bill Gates is smiling."

CHAPTER EIGHT

THE ROAD AHEAD

Gates has guided Microsoft and its 27,000 employees to such heights that the company's annual net revenue approaches $15 billion. Currently the wealthiest individual in the world, Gates's personal fortune nears the $100 billion mark, an unheard-of plateau.

Despite his incredible success, Gates worries that another young, aggressive company will appear and surpass Microsoft in the same way that Microsoft surpassed to the rest of the computer industry in the 1980s and 1990s. "If you slow down even a little bit . . . someone else can come in and take the lead," he asserts. His belief has obviously trickled down to his subordinates, for one of his vice presidents cautions that "no matter how good your product, you are only eighteen months away from failure."

For instance, Gates pushed Microsoft to implement the Digital Nervous System years before most companies considered the idea. A digital nervous system is designed to instantly produce necessary information, and in his opinion, in the next century the businesses that can access information the quickest will hold the upper hand. He intends to maintain his position at the summit of the computer industry by adapting his company to the new system.

As he writes in his 1999 book, *Business @ the Speed of Thought*, "The successful companies of the next decade will be the ones that use digital tools to reinvent the way they work. These companies will make decisions quickly, act efficiently and directly touch their customers in positive ways. . . . A digital nervous system will let you do business at the speed of thought—the key to success in the twenty-first century."

Gates explains in his earlier book *The Road Ahead* that he heeds the lessons of prior businessmen who soared to the top, only to stumble when they eased their effort or lost their edge. For instance, Ken Olsen, the founder of the first successful computer firm, Digital Equipment Corporation, scoffed at the notion that smaller computers would become a fixture in individual homes and refused to enter the PC market.

Gates with the French version of his book,
The Road Ahead

"Success is a lousy teacher," writes Gates. "It seduces smart people into thinking they can't lose. And it's an unreliable guide to the future. What seems the perfect business plan or latest technology today may soon be as out-of-date as the eight-track tape player, the vacuum-tube television, or the mainframe computer."

Gates intends to avoid those pitfalls and to keep Microsoft at the top. Though he takes pride in his role of making the PC available for the buying public, he knows that change and innovation constantly bring new products and fresh challenges. "It's a little scary that as computer technology has moved ahead there's never been a leader from one era who was also a leader in the next. Microsoft has been a leader in the PC era. So from a historical perspective, I guess Microsoft is disqualified from leading in the highway era of the Information Age. But I want to defy historical tradition. Somewhere ahead is the threshold dividing the PC era from the highway era. I want to be among the first to cross over when the moment comes."

As a daily reminder that he must aggressively pursue new avenues, Gates keeps a framed autographed picture of industrialist Henry Ford on the wall behind his desk. Gates believes that Ford slackened after his initial success in making the automobile affordable to the average family, and thereby permitted General Motors to supplant Ford as the leading automobile manufacturer. He vows that the same phenomenon will not occur at Microsoft. As one company executive, Jeff Raikes, mentioned to *Fortune* magazine, "It's etched in our brains: Don't get complacent."

The drive that propelled Gates to the top places him in an enviable position for the future. A rival executive told *The New Yorker* magazine that "Now is the time to conquer new foes, plunder new lands," and added that Gates will not hesitate to charge ahead. To those who contend that Gates is little more than a ruthless businessman who shoves other companies out of the way, the executive said, "To hold war councils and to design strategies with the explicit aim of crushing an opponent—this is very American. You know, Mother Teresa is not going to build the broadband network of the future."

Gates already began to map out his future at Microsoft by creating a new role for himself in January 2000. He announced that he would become the company's Chief Software Architect and made Steve Ballmer the company's Chief Executive Officer. Gates said in a statement that he was "returning to what I love most—focusing on technologies for the future."

TOMORROW'S INTERNET

Like every other computer enthusiast, Gates realizes that the next commercial empires will be built on the information superhighway, which Gates believes "will transform our culture as dramatically as Gutenberg's [printing] press did the Middle Ages." Rather than search for material in libraries or leaf through magazines, Gates explains that "any piece of information you want should be available to you" as quickly as as the time it takes to log onto the network. Vast systems

*Gates and Ballmer take a break
from Microsoft business.*

will eventually link together every computer in the world to ensure a constant stream of information.

He writes in *The Road Ahead* that we have seen merely the beginning of the information superhighway and heralds the enticing possibilities to come. "You will be able to stay in touch with anyone, anywhere, who wants to stay in touch with you; to browse through any of thousands of libraries, day or night. Your misplaced or stolen camera will send you a message telling you exactly where it is, even if it's in a different city."

Should you want to attend a certain performance at the local theater, you can find out if tickets remain and whether the route from your home to the theater is free of accidents. You can instantly check your child's school attendance and grade records, whether your shirts are ready at the dry cleaners, and if anyone has a superb recipe for beef stew. Instead of watching a television program when the networks schedule it, you will be able to watch the program when it is convenient for you, and you will be able to access any movie made by Hollywood.

Gates compares the information superhighway to a marketplace where individuals "will sell, trade, invest, haggle, pick stuff up, argue, meet new people, and hang out. . . . Think of the hustle and bustle of the New York Stock Exchange or a farmers' market or of a bookstore full of people looking for fascinating stories and information. All manner of human activity takes place, from billion-dollar deals to flirtations. Many transactions will involve money, tendered in digital form rather than currency. Digital information of all kinds, not just as money, will be the new medium of exchange in this market."

He sees a time when the PC will either control or absorb other communication devices in the home, such as the television, fax machine, and telephone. He predicts computers will be in living rooms and will most likely be contained in something similar to a cable converter box. Just as Microsoft provided the basic operating systems for most PCs with Windows, he wants his company to provide the standard operating systems for the information superhighway. In Gates's vision, every home and business will be linked together in this vast superhighway, all using a Microsoft operating system.

Another area in which Gates has focused his research is the wallet PC, a small computer-like device that could be carried in a purse or a back pocket. A wallet PC would give an individual instant access to the information superhighway and all its advantages, and could transfer funds from personal bank accounts to pay for purchases. He foresees a cashless future where consumers use a wallet PC instead of coins and paper currency. Whenever anyone uses the wallet PC, the manufacturer would receive a service fee, just as a bank does today. Consequently, Gates has forged alliances with financial institutions so that Microsoft will obtain those fees.

His competitors will be firms that offer access to the information superhighway, such as cable companies, AT&T, and America Online, and any-

Gates discusses hand-held computers at the Computer Electronics Show in 1998.

one who attempts to develop a new operating system to challenge Gates's Windows, such as Apple and IBM. Financial firms in conjunction with computer manufacturers will also compete.

Gates, who expects the entire information superhighway to be available around 2005, relishes the next decade because of the dizzying changes that will occur. "The pace of its evolution is so rapid that a description of the Internet as it existed a year or even six months ago might be seriously out of date."

He is just as intrigued by the potential for vast changes in the information superhighway as he was by the dawn of the PC. "I'm still thrilled by the feeling that I'm squinting into the future and catching that first revealing hint of revolutionary possibilities. I feel incredibly lucky that I am getting the chance to play a part in the beginning of an epochal change for a second time."

Gates has already impressed some analysts. Jeffrey Tarter, who produces a newsletter about the computer industry, told *Fortune* magazine that Gates has established a base in areas that his competitors have missed. "Gates recognizes that the most important transactions on the information highway won't be e-mail or reading the newspaper but commercial ones. People write a lot more checks than letters, don't they?"

GATES'S FUTURE

Gates claims that he will maintain his exhausting schedule with Microsoft through his forties, and then focus on charitable efforts. He adds that he will eventually give away ninety percent of his wealth so that his family will not have to manage such an enormous financial empire, and because he doesn't "believe in kids having too much money."

Until then, he will eagerly jump into the computer wars, trying to create improved products, face more complex problems, and make additional profits. He anticipates a few failures along the way, but expects the successes to vastly outnumber the problems.

In an interview with *Fortune* magazine, Gates peered into the future. "I'm sure we'll have failures. Some will be visible, and some won't. But we can afford to make a few mistakes now, and we can't afford *not* to try. Because of the scope of opportunity, and with shareholders' expectations for us to keep sales and profits growing, everything's about big horizons at Microsoft now. But, hey, we *can* tackle big horizons. We're *expected* to tackle big horizons. We *love* big horizons."

> **We can afford to make a few mistakes now, and we can't afford *not* to try.**

CHRONOLOGY

1955   William Henry Gates III is born in Seattle, Washington on October 28.

1967   Gates enters Lakeside School.

1969   Along with his computer friends at Lakeside, Gates works for Computer Center Corporation.

1972   Schedules classes for Lakeside; close friend, Kent Evans, is killed.

1973   Forms Traf-O-Data with Paul Allen; works on hydroelectric dams for TRW; graduates from Lakeside School; enters Harvard University.

1975   Reads the *Popular Electronics* article about the Altair 8800; forms Micro-Soft with Paul Allen.

1976   Writes "Open Letter to Hobbyists."

1977   Closes deals with Tandy Corporation

and Apple Computers to install BASIC; wins lawsuit against Pertec.

1978   Signs contract with Kazuhiko Nishi to distribute Microsoft products in East Asia; moves company headquarters to Bellevue, Washington.

1980   Agrees to develop operating system and a computer language for IBM.

1982   Agrees to develop programs for Apple's Macintosh computers.

1983   Paul Allen retires due to illness.

1985   Celebrates Microsoft's tenth anniversary; releases Windows 1.0.

1986   Moves Microsoft to its campus in Redmond, Washington; announces that the company is going public.

1988   Introduces Windows 2.0; is sued by Apple for illegally copying features of its operating system.

1990   Introduces Windows 3.0 to much acclaim.

1994   Marries Melinda French; signs a contract with Scholastic Corporation to develop products for the youth market.

1995   Forges an alliance with Chemical Bank to move Microsoft into the world of finance.

1996   Forms a partnership with the National Broadcasting Company to produce CD-

ROM software, online news services, and television programs; daughter Jennifer is born.

1997 Introduces Microsoft's Internet browser, Explorer 4.0; Gates and family move into their luxurious home on the shore of Lake Washington.

1999 Microsoft and the Department of Justice continue to battle in the courtroom over whether Microsoft holds a monopoly; Publishes his book *Business @ the Speed of Light*; son Rory John Gates is born in Seattle on May 23.

2000 Steps down as Chief Executive Officer at Microsoft; becomes the company's Chief Software Architect.

A NOTE ON SOURCES

One of the first sources to read is Gates's own 1995 book, *The Road Ahead* (New York: Viking, 1995). A combination autobiography and glimpse into the future, the book provides an illuminating view of Gates. Extremely helpful to my research were several recent biographies. James Wallace and Jim Erickson's *Hard Drive: Bill Gates and the Making of the Microsoft Empire* (New York: HarperBusiness, 1992) includes useful material about Gates's formation of his computer empire; Stephen Manes and Paul Andrews deliver a thoughtful examination of Gates from childhood on in their book *Gates* (New York: Simon & Schuster, 1994); and Daniel Ichbiah adds helpful information in *The Making of Microsoft* (Rocklin, California: Prima Publishing, 1993). For a more critical examination of Gates, read Jennifer Edstrom and Marlin Eller's *Barbarians Led by*

Bill Gates (New York: Henry Holt and Company, 1998).

Many superb magazine articles have profiled Bill Gates through the years, particularly those in *Fortune*, *Business Week*, and *The New Yorker*. Among the best are Richard Brandt, "The Billion-Dollar Whiz Kid," *Business Week*, April 13, 1987, pp. 68–76; Alan Deutschman, "Bill Gates' Next Challenge," *Fortune*, December 28, 1992, pp. 30–44; *Playboy* interview with Bill Gates, December 8, 1994; Kathy Rebello, "Microsoft: Bill Gates's Baby Is on Top of the World. Can It Stay There?" *Business Week*, February 24, 1992, pp. 60–65; Brent Schlender, "What Bill Gates Really Wants," *Fortune*, January 16, 1995, pp. 34–63; and John Seabrook, "E-Mail from Bill," *The New Yorker*, January 10, 1994, pp. 48–61.

FOR MORE INFORMATION

BOOKS

Boyd, Aaron. *Smart Money: The Story of Bill Gates*. Morgan Reynolds Incorporated, 1995.

Dickinson, Joan D. *Bill Gates: Billionaire Computer Genius*. Enslow Publishers, Inc., 1997.

Lesinski, Jeanne M. *Bill Gates*. Lerner Publications Company, 2000.

Woog, Adam. *Bill Gates*. Lucent Books, 1999.

ORGANIZATIONS AND INTERNET SITES

Bill and Melinda Gates Foundation
http://www.gatesfoundation.org/
Learn about the many ways Bill Gates and his wife are helping to improve people's lives.

The Gates Operating System
**http://www.pathfinder.com/time/gates/
index.html**
The *Time* magazine cover story on Gates from its
January 13, 1997 issue.

Information on the Computer Industry
**http://www.corpwatch.org/trac/feature/micr
osoft**
Interviews with analysts about their views of
Gates, Microsoft, and other industry companies
and leaders.

Microsoft Corporate Information
http://www.microsoft.com
The official site of Microsoft includes pages devot-
ed to Bill Gates, company products and developments, quotes from executives, and legal
information.

INDEX

ABOUT THE AUTHOR

John F. Wukovits is a junior high school teacher and writer from Trenton, Michigan, who specializes in history and biography. He has written a biography of World War II commander Admiral Clifton Sprague for the Naval Institute Press and biographies of Barry Sanders, Tim Allen, Jack Nicklaus, Vince Lombardi, Anne Frank, and Jim Carrey for the teenage market. A graduate of the University of Notre Dame, Wukovits is the father of three daughters—Amy, Julie, and Karen.